A Line in the Sand

A Line in the Sand

by

Guillermo Verdecchia and Marcus Youssef

Talonbooks

1997

Published with the assistance of the Canada Council.

Talonbooks
#104—3100 Production Way
Burnaby, British Columbia
Canada V5A 4R4

Typeset in New Baskerville and printed and bound in Canada by
Hignell Printing.

First Printing: September, 1997

Talonbooks are distributed in Canada by General Distribution
Services, 30 Lesmill Road, Don Mills, Ontario, Canada, M3B 2T6;
Tel: (416) 445-3333; Fax: (416) 445-5967.

Talonbooks are distributed in the U. S. A. by General Distribution
Services Inc., 85 Rock River Drive, Suite 202, Buffalo, New York,
U.S.A., 14207-2170; Tel.: 1-800-805-1083; Fax: 1-800-481-6207.

Canadian Cataloguing in Publication Data
Verdecchia, Guillermo.
 A line in the sand

 A play.
 ISBN 0-88922-375-0

 I. Youssef, Marcus. II. Title.
 PS8593.E67L56 1997   C812'.54   C97-910724-5
 PR9199.3.V45L56 1997

For
Souad and Mark Moussa, in memory
—M.Y

Alejandro and Roberto Verdecchia
—G.V.

Thanks to: Karim Alrawi, Robin Benger, Mordecai Briemberg, Dennis Foon, Urjo Kareda, Laila Maher, Doug and Janette Pirie, George Youssef, Roleene Youssef; Norman Armour and Darren Copeland at Wireless Grafitti; Roy Surette at Touchstone Theatre and Donna Spencer at the Firehall Theatre; friends on and around Commercial Drive.

Special thanks to Tamsin Kelsey for tremendous support, patience and more; to Amanda Fritzlan for love, wisdom and level-headed advice; and Zakaraiya Youssef, born the night of our first preview. The authors also wish to acknowledge the invaluable contributions of the actors who performed in the Vancouver and Toronto productions.

A Line in the Sand was first produced in Vancouver at the New Play Centre in April of 1995 with the following cast:

Mercer	Vincent Gale
Sadiq	Camyar Chai
Colonel	Tom Butler
Norman	Norman Armour
Marcus Youssef	Marcus Patrick Youssef

Directed by Guillermo Verdecchia
Stage Managed by Michel Bisson
Designed by Adrian Muir

The play was revised and presented in Toronto at the Tarragon Theatre in April of 1996 with the following cast:

Mercer	Vincent Gale
Sadiq / Actor 2	Camyar Chai
Colonel / Actor 1	Tom Butler

Directed by Guillermo Verdecchia
Stage Managed by Kristen Gilbert
Designed by Glenn Davidson and Sue Lepage

The text that follows is from the Tarragon production.

Characters

MERCER, a Canadian soldier, approximately 20 years old
SADIQ, a Palestinian boy, approximately 17 years old
COLONEL, a Canadian soldier, at least 45 years old

Setting

The play is set in the desert just outside of Doha, Qatar, during Operation Desert Shield in the Persian Gulf in the late fall of 1990.

Act One

Scene One

MERCER is alone in the sand. His gun is out of reach. He splashes water from a canteen onto his face. SADIQ enters.

SADIQ:
Hey.

Mister. Man.

Hey. Military man.

MERCER stops.

MERCER:
Paul James Mercer. Private. 3rd Battalion, Royal Canadian Regiment. I am serving with the multinational coalition—

SADIQ:
It is OK. I have no gun.

MERCER:
Who are you?

SADIQ:
No one. I come in peace.

SADIQ sets his large nylon bag down and MERCER grabs his gun.

MERCER:
Get your fucking hands in the air!

SADIQ:

Please, please, it is OK—

MERCER:

I said, get 'em in the air!

SADIQ:

Don't shoot!

MERCER:

Shut up! Who the fuck are you?

SADIQ:

Mohammed Sadiq Hamid. Not soldier—Palestinian.
Look, look, nice, nice, no gun, no gun...

MERCER:

You're trespassing. This is a militarized zone under the
jurisdiction of the United Nations.

SADIQ:

No soldiers here. Only water and sand.

MERCER:

It's close enough.

SADIQ:

As you say.

MERCER:

So fuck off.

SADIQ:

Please, just small moment.... It's OK, I got what you
want.

MERCER:
Why's your English so good?

SADIQ:
I study extra in school.

MERCER:
What for?

SADIQ:
My uncle in City of Kansas. Owns many homes. Soon I will go. To America.

MERCER:
You Palestinians are the guys we're supposed to watch out for. Might try to car bomb our air base.

SADIQ:
Not me, Military Man. I don't care about that.

MERCER:
You part of the uprising, that—uh—in-ti-faggot thing?

SADIQ:
Intifada.

MERCER:
Whatever the hell it's called.

SADIQ:
That is West Bank, Israel. Is one thousand kilometre from here.

MERCER:
Saddam is going to get his ass kicked, you know.

SADIQ:
   You are right. Big tough American soldier like you—
   must win for sure—

MERCER:
   I'm not American, kid, I'm Canadian.

SADIQ:
   Oh. Canadian. Yes! The peacekeepers. Frère Jacques,
   Frère Jacques. Dormez-vous…. They teach us this song
   in school…

MERCER:
   Oh, yeah.

SADIQ:
   Oui. It is big part of your culture, yes? You speak
   French, yes?

MERCER:
   No, I'm from Vancouver.

SADIQ:
   I could not live like that, all the snow…. I like sun—get
   dark in the Canada for eight months in year, yes?

MERCER:
   No.

SADIQ:
   You lying. I know, we learn all about the Canada.
   Special textbook donated from your government. We
   look in book and laugh at clothes you people wear. You
   cut big bear open and climb inside.

   Your skin is like snow, Canada. Maybe you going to
   melt.

So tell me, what would you like. I got much for sell to
Canadian soldier.

MERCER:

Like what?

SADIQ:

(cautiously pulls photographs from his bag) Pictures,
photograph, look at this.

MERCER:

(Relaxes, finally puts gun down) Holy shit.

SADIQ:

Good hey? Very popular with American soldier. Good
for Canadian, too huh. And this.

MERCER:

Fuck—where do you get this?

SADIQ:

My boss, Salim. He is big merchant, buy from
Americans in Cairo. They sell to US Army. For men on
base. Is good for Canada too, hey. You like?

MERCER:

Fuck, this heat.

SADIQ:

It's OK, Vancouver?

MERCER:

Yeah, yeah. I'm fine.

SADIQ:

(Hands MERCER water bottle) Here.

MERCER:
Fucking desert. Fucking sun.

SADIQ:
Very good price.

MERCER:
How much you want?

SADIQ:
How many?

MERCER:
Just the one's I saw—

SADIQ:
Twenty dollars.

MERCER:
All right.

Here.

They exchange.

SADIQ:
What is this? This purple, with bird eating fish. Is no good.

MERCER:
It's two ten dollar bills. Twenty bucks.

SADIQ:
Ha. You can't fool me, Vancouver. I must go to City of Kansas. Need hard money to get there.

MERCER:
That's as hard as you're going to get. Canadian dollars.

SADIQ:

Is no good to me.

MERCER:

Why the fuck not?

SADIQ:

Salim, my boss, he say everything must be American dollars. When I start, I sell cigar to skinny black soldier for Bangladeshi dollar, Salim just laugh. Make me pay.

MERCER:

Well, Canada's not fucking Bangladesh, pal.

SADIQ:

Very big price—from Cuba.

MERCER:

I'll give you forty. It's worth like thirty-five US.

SADIQ:

Now we talk turkey.

MERCER:

Right on, brother.

SADIQ:

You want more? Different? I have cigar, cigarettes. Marlboro. American Camel.

MERCER:

Don't smoke.

SADIQ:

Radio? I have radio.

MERCER:
Got one.

SADIQ:
CD. Michael Jackson

MERCER:
No.

SADIQ:
Tape for video—Madonna. Like a Virgin. Nice shirt,
blue jean from Guess, what you want, I can get.

MERCER:
I got everything I need on the base.

SADIQ:
Canada Dry One.

MERCER:
How'd you know that?

SADIQ:
I know many things.

MERCER:
Right. You staying here?

SADIQ:
No, I go to Kansas.

MERCER:
I mean here, the beach. You staying?

SADIQ:
You want I should stay?

MERCER:

No, I want you should go.

SADIQ:

This beach private of GI Vancouver?

MERCER:

Look, nothing personal. I'm just getting a little bored. This is my time off.

SADIQ:

Is OK, I have work to do. You want more picture you know where to find.

Scene Two

SADIQ:
Welcome back, Canada Dry One.

MERCER:
How's it going?

SADIQ:
Special today—*(holds up perfume bottle)* Obsession. Very nice for send to girlfriend.

MERCER:
No, thanks...

SADIQ:
Yes, you very smart. Not real Obsession, is only from Cairo.

> *Pause.*

You want more picture? Very expensive. More than before.

MERCER:
Right.

SADIQ:
For you, I get real good. Best price.

MERCER:
Yeah? Let's see.

> *SADIQ pulls out photographs. MERCER studies them intently as Sadiq shows him each one.*

No. No. No. Yes. No. No. Yes. *(Beat)*

This woman—she looks dead.

SADIQ:
    Pretend. Acting.

MERCER:
    How do you know?

SADIQ:
    Salim, my boss, he say no one gets hurt.

MERCER:
    Better than the real thing, eh?

SADIQ:
    I do not understand.

MERCER:
    Just a joke, kid. How much for the three?

SADIQ:
    One hundred US dollars.

MERCER:
    Forget it, man.

SADIQ:
    What you say, boss. *(he begins to put photographs away)*

MERCER:
    I'll give you fifty. Canadian.

SADIQ:
    Purple fish? For beg and steal from Salim? Then I
    never go to Kansas.

MERCER:
    Seventy-five.

SADIQ:
Ho, for you, OK. Seven five.

MERCER:
Special offer, huh?

SADIQ:
What?

MERCER:
You're giving me a deal, eh?

SADIQ:
What is your name?

MERCER:
Mercer.

SADIQ:
Mercer. I am Sadiq.

MERCER:
Sadiq?

SADIQ:
Sadiq. Yes, we make deal. Seven five purple fish.

MERCER:
Here, Sadiq.

Hands SADIQ money.

SADIQ:
Look, I have nice envelope for picture. Customer is always right.

MERCER:
  Yeah.

  Pause.

MERCER:
  What are you doing?

SADIQ:
  Look at water. Beautiful.

  My brother is over there *(he points)*. In West Bank. I not
  see since I am twelve. You have brother?

MERCER:
  How old are you?

SADIQ:
  Sixteen.

MERCER:
  Sixteen, huh?

SADIQ:
  And you?

MERCER:
  I'm twenty.

SADIQ:
  I am seventeen very soon. One—two month. You
  skinny to be soldier.

MERCER:
  What?

SADIQ:

> You very skinny. Americans soldier much more, you know, with beef. Canadian soldier is much less beef, yes?

MERCER:

> Well, I don't know if skinny is the word I'd use but— we're not all the same, you know.

SADIQ:

> You—different. How you different?

MERCER:

> I don't know.
>
> I went to university.

SADIQ:

> I do not understand.

MERCER:

> Most of these guys, they join up 'cause they got nothing else. Or they want a free education. Not me.

SADIQ:

> Why you join?

MERCER:

> I wanted to get my shit together. I was at Queen's University. What a fucking waste of time.

SADIQ:

> School. Puh. School is no good.

MERCER:

> You're telling me.

SADIQ:

My brother real good in school. Always top. Now he is in prison.

MERCER:

Oh yeah?

SADIQ:

Here I learn real life. But my father, he know I not go to school, he would break my throat.

MERCER:

Fuck. When I quit school and joined up, my father freaked.

SADIQ:

Freak?

MERCER:

He got really angry.

SADIQ:

For why?

MERCER:

He's a government big-shot. Makes him look bad, his son's a stupid soldier.

SADIQ:

Yes. You like me.

MERCER:

What?

SADIQ:

You...like...me.

MERCER:
No I don't.

SADIQ:
No, I say, "You like me."

MERCER:
I don't even know you.

SADIQ:
No, no. Like me. For angry father you join army—come to Qatar. Me also. Work for Salim and go to Kansas.

MERCER:
No. I didn't join because of him.

SADIQ:
Then why you join?

MERCER:
I told you. I wanted discipline.

A few months ago there was this thing that happened in Canada with our Indians, they blockaded this town—I watched it on TV at our base in Germany. This soldier—some stupid private—standing at the barricade while this Indian's calling him the worst kind of shit. Guy's spit landing right in his face—soldier didn't move a muscle, not even a twitch. Two inches away, injun's screaming, calling him goof, fuck-wad, cocksucker—

But nothing could touch that guy. That's why I joined.

SADIQ:
Why Indian so for angry?

MERCER:

> Oh, fuck, I don't know. It was some fucking golf course
> they wanted or something.

SADIQ:

> And mother? She afraid you go to war—be shoot and
> killed?

MERCER:

> Fuck off.

SADIQ:

> Why you anger Vancouver? The heat not good to you.
> You should go slow. Rest. Stay in base.

MERCER:

> You should fuck off.

SADIQ:

> I go. You want more picture. I come back three days.

MERCER:

> I won't be here so don't fucking bother.

Scene Three

SADIQ:
You say you will not come back.

MERCER:
Changed my mind. OK?

SADIQ:
OK.

MERCER:
Look, I'm sorry I weirded out on you last time.

SADIQ:
I have pictures. I have made selection.

MERCER:
Oh yeah?

SADIQ:
Yes. *(shows MERCER pictures)*

MERCER:
Fuck.

SADIQ:
You soldiers stay here a while, I make it to Kansas City no time. Flash. 6 months.

MERCER:
Must be your personal stash.

SADIQ:
I do not understand.

MERCER:

Ah, c'mon, don't tell me you don't sneak a quick pull over these in the back of your boss' tent.

SADIQ:

I not look at picture. They are not for me.

MERCER:

I can't get 'em out of my head. During exercises, on watch—I get up in the middle of the night, sneak 'em out of my tent in my shirt. I go to the fucking latrine for Christ's sake.

I haven't seen my girlfriend in a long fucking time. Based in Germany. But these pictures, they're something else.

SADIQ:

Top quality.

MERCER:

How much for these?

SADIQ:

Today, for you—fifty purple fish.

MERCER:

Deal.

SADIQ:

Deal.

MERCER:

Listen, these are way better than what we can get on the base. It's all Playboy and lacy shit. I'll meet you here once a week and buy the hardest stuff you can get your hands on.

SADIQ:
 You buy every week?

MERCER:
 Yeah.

SADIQ:
 Yes, this is good, Mercer.

MERCER:
 Good. It's a deal then.

SADIQ:
 Deal.

MERCER:
 Great.

SADIQ:
 Very good.

 You are not so white today. Gold, like the sun. Look. I
 am so brown. Your nose straight. And your hair.
 Harrison Ford.

 One time I go to the hair cutter in my neighborhood,
 in Doha. Stupid ass. Say I want him to make my hair
 straight. Like movie star I tell him. I have money. I will
 pay you to do it. I know it is possible. I read about it in
 magazines. But he laugh at me, says, Sadiq, you always
 want to be somebody else. You should know, he says, all
 the other boys, they laugh at you, so worried about how
 you look, talking about America and movie stars. I do
 that to your hair, your father, he would kill me. He will
 say I am traitor to the Arabs, to Palestine, make people
 not go to my store.

MERCER:
Here.

> *Hands SADIQ money.*

SADIQ:
More purple fish?

MERCER:
Don't tell anyone. Other soldiers.

SADIQ:
What?

MERCER:
About this. What I told you before. Everything.

SADIQ:
Yes. *(he pockets money)* We have secret.

Scene Four

SADIQ:

My Uncle and his wife, when they get to America, right
away, they change their names. Here, they Souad and
Maher Moussa, but there, no, they Sue and Mike
Marshall. He play baseball. In big league.

MERCER:

Your uncle plays pro ball?

SADIQ:

Yes?

MERCER:

Your uncle—he plays professional baseball?

SADIQ:

Oh, no. Mike Marshall play baseball. Pitcher for twins
of Min-e-soda. My uncle, Maher, he name himself for
Mike Marshall. And Souad, she wanted to name
Talullah, like Tallulah Bankhead, star from movie. But
Maher is big guy, say to Souad—Mike Marshall wife
name Sue Marshall, good for her, good for you, too.

Many years Uncle Mike work very hard for rich
American serving dinner in hotel restaurant. Souad
clean room. They save all their money, buy house in
bad part of city. Then they rent to black people. Make
more money and buy more house. Keep going until
Maher, he is Mike, rich guy in Kansas. Salim, he
promise I make enough selling to soldiers during the
war, he will send me to Uncle in America. He will make
sure.

MERCER:

Sadiq.

SADIQ's turns to face MERCER. MERCER takes photograph.

SADIQ:
You have camera.

MERCER:
I do.

SADIQ:
Why?

MERCER:
To take pictures. You know.

SADIQ:
Of?

MERCER:
Everything. The desert.

SADIQ:
You have flash build in?

MERCER:
No.

SADIQ:
Is no good. Salim, my boss—

MERCER:
I know he's your boss, you say that every time you say his fucking name.

SADIQ:
Salim, he have small camera, like this. Excellent picture. Flash build in. Motor for film. All automatic.

MERCER:
Those are just for snap shots. They're toys.

SADIQ:
Take good picture. I see them. Good colours bright.
Flash for inside.

MERCER:
This camera lets me control everything. Shutter speed,
aperture. Those little ones—say you're backlit right?
You're in front of a window and there's a lot of light
streaming in. Well, with those little ones the camera
gets confused and underexposes your face. It comes
out in shadow.

SADIQ:
No, he have flash build in.

MERCER:
Right.

SADIQ:
Is good camera. Take good pictures.

MERCER:
Well, this one takes better pictures. Trust me.

SADIQ:
OK. I trust you.

Here. Take picture of me.

*SADIQ begins to pose; MERCER takes
photographs. SADIQ's poses are based on
magazine images, impersonating models, movie
stars etc. He takes off his shirt for the last pose or
two.*

MERCER:
I should get going.

SADIQ:
You go back to base?

MERCER:
Yeah. So…

SADIQ:
Here. *(gives MERCER envelope)*

MERCER:
Great. And this for you. *(pays him)* All right, I'm outta here. See you in a week.

SADIQ:
Wait, Mercer.

You must go back now?

MERCER:
Yeah, I got work to do. I'm not on holiday, you know.

SADIQ:
For you. *(offers MERCER another envelope)*

MERCER:
What? What's this?

SADIQ:
For you. Extra.

MERCER:
I haven't got any more money.

SADIQ:
No. Just for you. Free. A gift. Today, I do very good, sell
much. I make you a gift.

MERCER:
You sure?

SADIQ:
Yes.

MERCER:
What's the catch?

SADIQ:
I do not understand.

MERCER:
What do you want in return? What's the catch?

SADIQ:
No. Gift. To you. From Sadiq.

MERCER:
Why?

SADIQ:
What why? You understand gift Vancouver?

MERCER:
Yes. I know what a gift is.

SADIQ:
OK.

MERCER:
Why?

SADIQ:
Why not?

MERCER:
(accepts second envelope) All right.

SADIQ:
Stay a little.

MERCER:
And do what?

SADIQ:
Tell me of America.

MERCER:
I gotta go. I'll see you in a week.

Scene Five

SADIQ:
(sings) Rudolph the Red Nosed Reindeer. Had a very tiny nose. And if you ever saw it, you would even say it glows.

We see on TV with Salim.

Merry Christmas, Mercer.

MERCER:
It's not 'til next week.

Pause.

SADIQ:
Tell me about base. Canada Dry One.

MERCER:
What about it?

SADIQ:
What you do.

MERCER:
Sweet dick.

SADIQ:
Sweet?

MERCER:
Nothing. It's totally boring.

SADIQ:
You lying. Top secret. I see jeeps, many soldiers run, planes. You practice?

MERCER:
Yeah, we practice, neutralize fucking sand dunes.
Broman's always cooking up some stupid little exercise
to keep us busy. Now that everything's all set up there's
nothing to do.

SADIQ:
Nothing?

A pause, MERCER watches the waves.

SADIQ:
On base you have telephone?

MERCER:
Yeah, of course. We have lots of phones.

SADIQ:
In America, everyone have two telephones in house. In
cars too. My family, never a telephone.

MERCER:
Oh well.

SADIQ:
Tell me about America.

MERCER:
Shit, Sadiq. Just shut up for a minute.

SADIQ:
Tell only a little.

MERCER:
I'm not American.

SADIQ:

But still you know. Tell me.

MERCER:

OK. First, it's not what you think. It ain't like TV.

SADIQ:

Salim, my boss, he have CNN. We see all sides about America.

MERCER:

Yeah, well, don't believe everything you see. This place you think you're going, it's not real, it's in your head. Your uncle Mike, I don't know what he told you.

SADIQ:

Uncle Mike say any person work hard in America they can be rich. Like him.

MERCER:

Fuck that shit. The guys in my regiment, most of their families got nothing. On welfare or farmers working their asses off. Everybody's got guns in the States, they're fucking maniacs. In Canada we got health care. In the States, you're poor and you have a heart attack, they don't fucking care, they'll turn you away from the hospital.

SADIQ:

My Uncle Mike, he say only lazy people are poor in America. If you work you can be rich.

MERCER:

What's this thing with being rich? Money doesn't help, you know. You think that having two TVs is going to do anything for you? Having a car, two cars, big cars, a big

house, lots of telephones, you think that's gonna solve
your problems? No way Jose. Let me tell you.

SADIQ:
I want to be rich.

Beat.

Everybody want to be rich.

MERCER:
Not everybody.

SADIQ:
You know hungry. Yes? You know hungry? No. Look at
my shoes, Vancouver. Two years, same shoes. My father,
he always moving, work different country, dream of his
homeland. Little money he make he give away. To
PLO. Stupid poor man work for rich fat man. All I
remember, poor, hungry, the same the same the same.
I want more. There is more to live.

MERCER:
OK, OK, whatever.

SADIQ:
I work make dream come true. I quit school. I will go.
You rich, Vancouver. You not know work. You know
nothing. You are a child.

MERCER:
Hey, I work, asshole. You don't know shit about me or
what I've done. You're the child around here.

SADIQ:
Is true. Little baby.

Silence.

SADIQ:

Mercer—I get angry, no reason. Sorry.

MERCER:

Stop fucking touching me. You're always touching me.

SADIQ:

I apologize. I do not want anger to you.

A pause.

My father this morning, he find hashish I have for to sell. He learn I not go to school. He shout and shout at me. I say nothing. He is a fool. I am angry to him not to you.

MERCER:

That's a total sob story. My heart bleeds.

SADIQ:

You forgive?

MERCER:

Massage my feet.

SADIQ:

Rub feet? Yes? I know how to good. I do for my sister. Her, how you say, blood...too close?

MERCER:

Don't talk.

A silence.

SADIQ:

I apologize?

Is good rub?

MERCER:
> Give me the pictures.

> *SADIQ gives MERCER envelope with pictures.*
> *Continues rubbing his foot. MERCER looks at*
> *pictures.*

SADIQ:
> Is good rub?

> You should see my father, Mercer. His hands are black from oil. And the smell.

> There are four hundred thousand people here in Qatar. Three hundred thousand like my father—idiot foreigner work to make oil men rich. Before they find oil here, these rich men, you know what they do? Dive for pearls. Yes. Jump off old boats, swim and dig and hold their breath until they go blue. Every day, up and down, up and down, dig, swim, dig, swim. But now they are rich.

> My father says I am a fool. We need these men. They are our friends. These rich Arabs will help us win our home. Oh, he is thick. There is no oil in Palestine, only sand. When Palestine comes we will only stay here, like the Pakistanis and Indians he works with, so far from our home it will not matter that we have one.

> My father knows I will go to Uncle Mike in Kansas City. Fly across the ocean. TWA. If he tries to stop me I will say—look how much money I make working for Salim. And you know how I get it? Yes. Just like they say. From American soldier. GI Joe. Bombing and killing your brothers and sisters in Iraq.

> I live in Qatar. In America I will be born.

MERCER:
> Kiss my foot.

Scene Six

MERCER:
Sadiq!

SADIQ:
Mercer, hello. You are waiting?

MERCER:
A while. I couldn't get away yesterday. Fucking Broman.
So I came today. I didn't know whether you'd come by.

SADIQ:
No.

MERCER:
What?

SADIQ:
I am here.

MERCER:
You are. Me too.

SADIQ:
Yes. Here we are.

MERCER:
So you got some?

SADIQ:
What?

MERCER:
Pictures.

SADIQ:
> You want more picture?

MERCER:
> Yeah. We have a deal.

SADIQ:
> No. No picture left.

MERCER:
> Why not?

SADIQ:
> All sold. Very popular with soldier. Salim, my boss, he sell-out.

MERCER:
> None?

SADIQ:
> You have many picture already.

MERCER:
> We made a deal.

SADIQ:
> I have cassettes. Music. Metallica. Guns to Roses.

MERCER:
> I don't want any fucking cassettes.
>
> What fucking good are you? Jesus, I've been waiting out here for a fucking hour. You don't have any left.

SADIQ:
> No. I say already. No more picture.

MERCER:
Bullshit. Let me see your bag.

SADIQ:
Why?

MERCER:
Let me see.

SADIQ:
You don't believe?

MERCER:
No. Show me.

He tries to grab bag.

SADIQ:
No.

MERCER:
Open it!

What's this? Bullshit. Don't have any pictures. What are these eh? Lying little fuck.

SADIQ:
No, not for sale.

MERCER:
I'm not buying. I'm taking.

SADIQ:
Mercer, pictures, pictures. No good. Only picture. Why you want so many pictures?

MERCER:
What do you think, raghead?

SADIQ:
   You want for fuck? Pictures?

MERCER:
   That's right. I want for fuck. You know what that is?

SADIQ:
   Why picture?

MERCER:
   'Cause that's what I like.

SADIQ:
   You like.

MERCER:
   Right.

SADIQ:
   Why you do this to me Mercer?

MERCER:
   I didn't do anything.

SADIQ:
   Why you ask me to rub feet?

MERCER:
   What?

SADIQ:
   I go now.

MERCER:
   No, hey look. I'll pay you for these. Don't get all fucking touchy. You're the one that fucked up not me.

MERCER pays him. SADIQ starts to go.

Where you going? Stick around.

SADIQ:
You have pictures. What else you want now?

MERCER:
Nothing. I don't want anything.

SADIQ:
OK. I go.

MERCER:
Hey, fuck. Relax. Let's have a smoke or something.

SADIQ:
I have no more hash. Look if you don't believe.

MERCER:
No, OK. I believe you. Why you in such a hurry all of a sudden?

SADIQ:
I have work to do.

MERCER:
Fuck that. Come on, this is my time off.

SADIQ:
So?

MERCER:
So tell me something.

SADIQ:
What?

MERCER:

I don't know. You usually have a million things to say.
Tell me about your family.

SADIQ:

Why?

MERCER:

'Cause I want to know.

SADIQ:

No, you just want pictures.

MERCER:

OK, fuck off then.

SADIQ:

No, you fuck off. This is my beach too.

Silence.

We are six in my family. Father, mother, two sisters,
brother and me. I am youngest. My sisters both
married. Fatma, she is teacher. Leila, she have four
children. I am uncle. Mother is dead. My brother,
Hanni, he is killed in prison. Choke on tear gas, die.
Three years ago. So we are only four. But sisters are in
West Bank so we are only Father and me.

MERCER:

Holy shit.

SADIQ:

I very missing Leila, Fatma. Already four year. You have
brother sister?

MERCER:

No, just the three of us.

A pause.

Two of us actually. Now.

My mother just died. Just before I met you.

SADIQ:
Mercer…I am sorry.

MERCER:
You didn't do anything.

SADIQ:
For mother.

MERCER:
She was in the hospital for a long time. A mental hospital. Twelve years. I only ever saw her at Christmas. She was a mess. She's better off dead.

The service was packed. Some church. Dad and all his big shot buddies from the ministry pretending they gave a shit. Telling me they were sorry. She was fucked. I wouldn't have recognized her if she'd climbed out of the coffin and told my father and me to go fuck ourselves. Jennifer was there, couldn't look at her. I always told her my mother was dead. Dad didn't say a word. Trying to act all serious and sad but inside he was dancing.

SADIQ:
When my mother die, I am little boy. No one tell me. For two, three week they say she is gone to her sister for visit. I find out from boys at school. Then I am angry. At mother for going. Then I am older, I get angry to father for tell lie.

50

MERCER:
Yeah.

My father was an asshole. Never around. Always at
work. When they put my mom in hospital he sent me
to boarding school. I was ten for fuck's sake.

SADIQ:
Is OK.

MERCER:
What?

SADIQ:
To be sad.

MERCER:
Well I'm not. I'm not anything. It's like nothing there.
Like a hole. It's just a hole. And it fucks me up 'cause
my mother is dead and I don't give a shit and you're
supposed to give a shit when your mom dies but I
don't.

SADIQ:
Where?

MERCER:
What?

SADIQ:
The hole. Here? *(indicates MERCER's abdomen)*

MERCER:
Yeah. *(SADIQ puts his hand on MERCER's stomach)*

SADIQ:
I know. You empty. Me too.

MERCER:
Yeah. Nothing.

SADIQ:
I know. We are child.

MERCER:
Yeah.

SADIQ:
You hurt.

MERCER:
(a whisper) Yeah.

SADIQ:
I know. Is OK.

Scene Seven

MERCER:

Sadiq, you should go to Canada. Not to the States, go
to Canada.

SADIQ:

No, my uncle can bring me to America. I have no
person in Canada.

MERCER:

My dad, he's a big bureaucrat, he could do something I
bet, he could get you in. Whatever. As a refugee or
something.

SADIQ:

Where I live in Canada, Mercer? In house with you and
your father?

MERCER:
No. I don't think so.

SADIQ:
Me too, I don't think so.

MERCER:

But we could work something out. I don't know. You
could visit at least. You'd like it. You ever seen snow?

SADIQ:
Snow? No.

MERCER:

Oh, yeah, come to Vancouver. I'll bring you. Sadiq, I
live on the ocean. And mountains. Trees Sadiq, trees so
big, you—

SADIQ:
Is too cold.

MERCER:
No, no, not where I live. I'll show you, I'll take you. It's cool, not too hot, not too cold. You can smell the ocean in the air. And there's these big trees covered in moss, the colour of rusted copper. It's quiet. And the waves. They're not like here. They crash all white onto the rocks. And there are purple starfish. And birds flying. Hawks and eagles riding thermals and sea gulls. And there's these Arbutus trees—their bark, it's the colour of your skin. And far off, far, the peaks of the mountains are white and the snow is there.

You have to come and visit.

SADIQ:
Will you go back to Canada after this?

MERCER:
After this?

A silence.

Crazy fucking world, eh?

I don't know. I guess. Depends on what happens. I guess I'm supposed to go back to Germany but, eventually, yeah, I think I'll go back to Canada. I don't know.

A pause.

SADIQ:
The war—when will it come?

MERCER:
Fuck if I know. Soon I hope. Deadline's in four days. Then it's up to the Americans.

SADIQ:
> Will you fight?

Mercer:

> No, no we don't do that kind of shit. We're the peace-keepers. Don't even know if our Hornets are gonna be allowed into combat. Typical Canada. Join the army but you ain't allowed to fight.

SADIQ:
> They have no choice.

MERCER:
> What?

SADIQ:
> They are not like you, Vancouver. Not want to be here.

MERCER:
> Who?

SADIQ:
> The Iraqis. The soldiers. They must sign up with army or go to prison. They have little food, just want to go home.

MERCER:
> No way, Sadiq. They're crack troops, elite. The Republican Guard, they beat the fucking Iranians, for Christ's sake. And you know how crazy they are.

SADIQ:
> No, I do not.

MERCER:
> You see on TV when the Ayatollah died? All those fuck-ing people. Like a million or whatever, grabbing at his

coffin. Fucking weird, man. Our Prime Minister—
Mulroney, if he died—I don't think anybody'd notice.

SADIQ:

You are a child.

MERCER:

Don't call me that. I know you're an Arab but you gotta
face the truth. It's like their—whadya call it—gee had
or whatever. It's a fucking holy war. If they get killed
fighting us they go straight to heaven.

SADIQ:

You think we just want to die? Because we are Muslim.
We don't have wives? Families? Children?

MERCER:

That doesn't matter. To them fundamentalists, life is
worth like nothing. Less than nothing. They'll blow
themselves up over anything. I mean, there's always
some kind of war here, all the time.

SADIQ:

From England and France.

MERCER:

What?

SADIQ:

For oil, come and make big mess.

MERCER:

You can't go blaming your problems on everybody else.

SADIQ:

Libya, 1986.

MERCER:
  What?

SADIQ:
  Americans bomb Tripoli. Many people dead. And
  Lebanon.

MERCER:
  I thought you didn't care about any of that shit.
  C'mon, Sadiq, you're out of here. You're going to
  Kansas.

SADIQ:
  This is my home. My people.

MERCER:
  It's not a personal thing Sadiq. I'm just doing my job.

SADIQ:
  Good job.

MERCER:
  Hey, I didn't think this fucking thing up you know. It's
  the way things go.

SADIQ:
  Destiny.

MERCER:
  Yeah. Fate. Life.

SADIQ:
  It will not happen.

MERCER:
  What?

SADIQ:

The war. Everything.

MERCER:

Yeah, maybe not. Who knows?

SADIQ:

Me. Tell me again Mercer, the purple fish and the
eagles with the snow so far on the mountains where I
visit you.

Act Two

A slash (/) indicates that ACTOR 2 begins speaking at that point. The use of different type is intended to suggest text that is under (lower in volume than) ACTOR 2's text.

ACTOR 1:
At 10:10 p.m. on January 16 of 1991, Prime Minister Brian Mulroney made the following speech to the House Of Commons:[1]

Mr. Speaker, honourable members will know that military action began in the Persian Gulf today, / as announced at 7 p.m. Eastern Standard Time.

ACTOR 2:
Population of Iraq: 18 million.

Cost of one Tomahawk missile: $1.4 million US.[2]

President Bush called me beforehand to apprise me that he had authorized such action. We understand at the moment that the participants of this first wave included forces from the United States, The United Kingdom, Saudi Arabia and Kuwait.

Estimated number of Tomahawk missiles fired at Iraq during first 2 weeks of war: 240[3]

59

ACTOR 1:
The fighting is a direct consequence of Saddam Hussein's determination to maintain his brutal occupation and illegal annexation of Kuwait in defiance of world opinion. He has chosen to ignore the numerous opportunities that were open to him to withdraw. He has had 167 days / since his illegal and brutal invasion of Kuwait on August 2, and 48 full days since the United Nations Security Council passed resolution 678 on November 29.
...

ACTOR 2:
Duration of Indonesian occupation of East Timor: 20 years.[4]

Number of UN sanctioned wars to liberate East Timor: 0.

Duration of Israeli occupation of West Bank: 28 years.

Number of UN sanctioned wars to liberate West Bank: 0.

Number of good Arabs in movie *True Lies*: 1.[5]

Estimated number of bad Arabs: 763,000.[6]

Lyrics to opening number from Walt Disney's *Aladdin*: "Oh, I come from a land, from a faraway place where the caravan camels roam; where they cut off your ear if they don't like your face. It's barbaric but hey, it's home."[7]

ACTOR 1:
Diplomacy has been given every chance to end this conflict peacefully, but regrettably has failed in the face of Saddam Hussein's intransigence.[8] That same intransigence and his indifference to the suffering of his own people, especially the children, / made it clear that sanctions alone were not going to force him to leave Kuwait....

ACTOR 2:
Estimated number of Iraqi children under the age of 5 dead as a result of the war, in the year following cessation of bombing: 150,000.[9]

Number of babies in Kuwait City incubators killed by Iraqis: 0.[10]

We have joined with other UN members in expelling Saddam Hussein from Kuwait by force. At this moment our CF-18s are flying combat air patrol in the Northern Persian Gulf, / protecting Canadian and allied ships and personnel in the Gulf and the Arabian Peninsula....

Number of CF-18's based in Persian Gulf: 24.[11]

Cost to taxpayer to purchase one CF-18: $35 million.[12]

Percentage of Canadian defence budget spent on peacekeeping: less than 1.[13]

ACTOR 1:
I profoundly regret, as I am sure, do
all members of this House, that it has
come to this. It is with no satisfaction
that we take up arms, because war is
always a tragedy, / but the greater
tragedy would have been for criminal
aggression to go unchecked.

I am sure that the safety of the Canadian
service men and women in the Gulf is
uppermost in the minds of all members.
Our hearts go out tonight to those families
with loved ones, fathers or mothers, sons
and daughters, and brothers and sisters,
on duty in the Persian Gulf. These
courageous men and women are braving
great danger in the defence of the values
and interests of their entire country. They
have our gratitude and respect, and
especially tonight our prayers....

ACTOR 2:
One thing Middle East and Somalia
have in common: Western support
for dictatorships.[14]

Another thing Middle East and
Somalia have in common: Huge
markets for Western arms.

One more thing Middle East and
Somalia have in common: Oil.[15]

Estimated number of Iraqi soldiers
killed during Gulf War: 100,000.[16]

ACTOR 2:
Number of American soldiers killed: 144.

Number of these American soldiers killed by friendly fire: 60.

Preferred weapon for attacking dug-in troops and heavy fortifications: Fuel Air Explosives.

Research for Fuel Air Explosive probably carried out at: McGill University, University of Toronto, University of Ottawa, University of British Columbia.[17]

Example of Fuel Air Explosive: Big Blue 82. The Big Blue 82 is a 15,000 pound bomb which explodes in a massive fireball. The pressure effects of Fuel Air Explosives, such as a Big Blue 82, approach those produced by low-yield nuclear weapons.[18] If one were dropped on the theatre right now...this entire neighbourhood? ... poof.

Act Three

Scene One

*A tent. MERCER sitting in a chair. The
COLONEL enters. MERCER jumps, unsteadily,
to attention.*

COLONEL:

At ease, Mercer. I got a pile of papers here to organize
so if you'll just give me a second. I'll tell you, there's
more goddamned paperwork in the Forces than I
don't know what. But if you don't fill out the forms,
you don't get paid. So, I fill out the forms. I filled out
forms all the way here. That generator make enough
noise for you? Should we tape record this?

*A squadron of planes take off. The noise is
deafening and lasts at least a minute.
COLONEL and MERCER both react to noise.
The COLONEL continues talking although we
can't hear what he is saying. The noise ends.*

COLONEL:

Here we go.

Reading.

I didn't know who he was or what he was doing there.
Raymond said they caught him sneaking around the
camp. It's pretty hard to say what all happened or in
what order. By the time I got there, he was already
pretty bad. Raymond was there and MasCorporal
Fortier. The Arab was—his head was all cut and bruised
and looked like his legs were bleeding too. He was tied
up. Raymond hit him with his riot baton and the Arab
would scream Canada Canada Canada. Raymond
laughed and said they'd been training him.

64

Somebody had a pistol out. It was lying on the table. They untied him, the Arab, they were poking him with the batons and making him walk around. He got over by the table and reached out to the gun. I grabbed his arm and tried to take it from him. We were pulling away at each other and the gun went off. It just went off. I didn't even know if it was loaded. I didn't know he'd been hit. He fell down. I can't say that I pulled the trigger. I don't know. He fell down and then Raymond and Fortier, or one of them, checked him and said he was dead. I don't remember much else after that.

COLONEL:
That's your statement. As taken by Lieutenant Broman. Those are your words.

MERCER:
Yes, sir.

COLONEL:
A fight. In the sand. You walked into this, he tries to grab a gun, you fight, a mistake, the gun goes off. He dies. That's basically what you're saying here.

MERCER:
Yes.

COLONEL:
Mercer, I have no opinions on the subject and nothing in particular that I want to hear but you are going to tell me exactly, precisely, all the nitty-gritty little fucking details of what happened.

MERCER:
It's pretty m-m-much...like that.

COLONEL:
That what?

MERCER:
Sir…like what you read, sir.

COLONEL:
What I read doesn't tell me anything Mercer. Just an outline, the surface. A couple of people in a dark tent. I want you to fill in the details.

A silence.

OK, let's start with something simple. What do you think of niggers, Mercer?

MERCER:
Sir?

COLONEL:
Niggers. What do you think of niggers? You have anything against them?

MERCER:
No sir.

COLONEL:
Pakis? Jews? Indians? You got anything against them?

MERCER:
No sir.

COLONEL:
Would you describe yourself as a racist?

MERCER:
No. I wouldn't sir.

COLONEL:

I'm just asking because it turns out that Raymond he's one of these White Power guys. Just want to know if you have anything to do with any of that.

MERCER:

No sir.

COLONEL:

Did you know that about Raymond? He talk to you about that at all?

MERCER:

Yes sir.

COLONEL:

He did? What did he say?

MERCER:

I don't remember exactly sir. I never paid much attention.

COLONEL:

He talk to you about Hitler and the purity of the race thing?

MERCER:

Sometimes, sir.

COLONEL:

But you never paid much attention.

MERCER:

I always thought Hitler was an asshole, sir.

COLONEL:

You think Raymond was an asshole?

MERCER:
No sir.

COLONEL:
But you weren't interested in that sort of thing?

MERCER:
No sir.

COLONEL:
You know if anybody else is into that stuff?

MERCER:
Can't say, sir. Don't know.

COLONEL:
Just Raymond then. Far as you know. What about
religion?

MERCER:
Pardon me sir?

COLONEL:
I want to know what religion you are Mercer. For the
forms. You NFR?

MERCER:
Yes sir.

COLONEL:
But you were brought up, what, Protestant?

MERCER:
Yes sir.

COLONEL:
You a lapsed Protestant then?

MERCER:
  Sir?

COLONEL:
  Just a little joke. You believe in God though Mercer?

MERCER:
  Uh...haven't given it much thought sir.

COLONEL:
  You haven't. Big idea. God. Takes some thinking. Not
  the kind of thing you can just decide about in a few
  minutes, eh Mercer. Right now though, would you say
  you're atheist or agnostic? *(a pause)* An agnostic would
  be somebody who—

MERCER:
  Is this for the forms sir?

COLONEL:
  Just idle curiosity Mercer.

MERCER:
  Right now sir, I'd have to say I'm an atheist.

COLONEL:
  No faith eh? No Big Plan out there as far as you're
  concerned. No Big Guy with a Big Beard.

  You had any sleep?

MERCER:
  No sir.

COLONEL:
  You want to get some air before we start?

MERCER:

No. Thank you sir.

COLONEL:

Something to eat?

MERCER:

No sir.

COLONEL:

Coffee? Smoke? Go ahead. Do you smoke?

MERCER:

No sir.

COLONEL:

I used to. Quit. About seventeen times. You don't want anything?

MERCER:

Not really sir.

COLONEL:

Where you from?

MERCER:

Vancouver. I'm from Vancouver, sir

COLONEL:

Nice there. Mountains and everything.

MERCER:

Yes sir it is.

COLONEL:

Rains a lot.

MERCER:
Fair bit.

COLONEL:
Doesn't get hot like this I bet?

MERCER:
N-n-n-o sir.

COLONEL:
Sun's a bitch isn't it?

MERCER:
Sir?

COLONEL:
Sun's a bitch. Get it? Sun's a bitch?

MERCER:
Ha. Yeah. Sun's a bitch all right sir.

COLONEL:
Vancouver.

MERCER:
Yes sir.

COLONEL:
I was in Vancouver few years ago. Got that nice market
down there on that island.

MERCER:
Granville Island?

COLONEL:
Yeah. That's it, that's by that goddamned clock isn't it?
That Gassy Clock thing that goes off every fifteen

minutes. Screeches like air brakes. Idiot tourists all gathered round the bloody thing, taking pictures.

MERCER:
I...n-don't know that clock sir.

COLONEL:
What part of town you live in?

MERCER:
W-w-west Vancouver, sir.

COLONEL:
What do you do there? You run around that Sea Wall thing?

MERCER:
That's pretty far from where I live sir. Don't do much. Used to ski a bit.

COLONEL:
Skiing. Skiing's nice. Whistler?

MERCER:
That's right sir.

COLONEL:
You engaged?

MERCER:
No sir.

COLONEL:
Just noticed your ring.

MERCER:
Just a ring sir.

COLONEL:
　You single then?

MERCER:
　Yes sir.

COLONEL:
　Family out there too?

MERCER:
　My father.

COLONEL:
　Right. Shit, I'm sorry. Your mother passed away. I'm
　sorry. Recent wasn't it?

MERCER:
　Yes, sir.

COLONEL:
　That's too bad. Terrible. *(pause)* How's your father
　taking it?

MERCER:
　My father, sir?

COLONEL:
　How's he taking it? Big blow for him.

MERCER:
　Yes sir.

　　A silence.

　Wasn't exactly a surprise sir. My m-mother'd been sick
　a long time.

COLONEL:
> That's always hard. Maybe better that way though. Would you say?

MERCER:
> Maybe sir.

COLONEL:
> Your father Mercer. What's he do?

MERCER:
> He's in government, sir. Associate Minister, I'm not exactly sure, Department of National Defence.

COLONEL:
> He's sort of my boss, isn't he?

MERCER:
> I guess.

COLONEL:
> Paul James Mercer. Born, 1939, in Gatineau, Quebec. Graduates at the age of seventeen, second in his class, from Upper Canada College. Full scholarship to McGill University. Bourassa Fellowship in Government. Law Degree at 24. Marries Susan Wainwright, 1963, a psychology MA. at McGill. First and only child, Paul Junior, born April, 1970. Susan becomes chronically depressed after the birth. Paul rises in the civil service. In 1989 is promoted to Assistant Deputy Minister with responsibility for UN Peacekeeping Operations.
>
> Homework.

MERCER:
> Yes sir.

COLONEL:
    You get along with your dad Mercer?

MERCER:
    Sure. Pretty much.

COLONEL:
    What about your mum?

MERCER:
    I did, I guess.

COLONEL:
    They tell me you're a good kid. Quiet.

    Pause.

    You went back for the funeral.

MERCER:
    Yes sir.

COLONEL:
    How was that?

MERCER:
    Sir?

COLONEL:
    How did you feel? At the funeral.

MERCER:
    Pardon me sir?

COLONEL:
    Were you upset? Did you cry?

MERCER:
  No sir.

COLONEL:
  No? Did you love your mother?

  A silence.

COLONEL:
  Mercer?

MERCER:
  …Yes sir.

COLONEL:
  How long was it since she'd lived with you and your
  father? You were what 6 or something?

MERCER:
  I was n-n-nine sir.

COLONEL:
  Nine. So you remember her ?

MERCER:
  I remember some.

COLONEL:
  What exactly?

MERCER:
  I remember her. How she'd look at me sometimes,
  smile and then keep on looking as if she could see
  right through me. I remember how she cried and cried
  one time after coming home from the hospital, she just
  cried because she spilt sugar all over the place when

she was trying to fill up the sugar bowl. I remember lots.

Do you want me to tell you more?

COLONEL:
No. That's fine. Was it hard for you to come back here? After.

MERCER:
Not really, sir.

COLONEL:
How've you been feeling?

MERCER:
Sir?

COLONEL:
In the past while, since your mother's death. All these things, you know, one on top of the other, would you say you've been under some stress?

MERCER:
I don't know sir.

COLONEL:
Were you upset at all, in any way, by your mother's death? Anything. I mean.... Dreams or whatever. It must have been pretty tough for you in some way.

Silence.

Even if you didn't really know her, she was your mother. I mean, it's possible that at the time, let's say at the funeral, you didn't feel anything, you were in a kind of shock, but after, later, maybe weeks later, you feel something. Anything. Not quite right. Would you say that you've been yourself since you've been here?

MERCER:
I don't know. It's different, but...

COLONEL:
Different?

MERCER:
Well, the heat sir. And the sand. I've never seen anything like this. But I'm a soldier sir.

COLONEL:
What does that mean to you? Being a soldier.

MERCER:
I follow orders sir. Discipline sir. Control. Keeping the peace...fighting for what's right.

COLONEL:
Whose orders you follow?

MERCER:
Officers' sir.

COLONEL:
Your officers give orders to mistreat that prisoner?

MERCER:
Prisoner?

COLONEL:
The Arab, Mercer. Did you receive orders as to how to deal with him?

MERCER:

It was understood sir, that, uh, p-p-p-prisoners were to be taught a lesson.

COLONEL:

How was this understood?

MERCER:

It was sir. It just was.

COLONEL:

Did anyone in particular say anything specifically about what should be done to the prisoner?

MERCER:

I don't think so.

COLONEL:

Let me ask you again. Who's orders specifically do you follow?

MERCER:

Sir, my my my superiors.

COLONEL:

You always had a stutter Mercer?

MERCER:

Sir?

COLONEL:

Stutter Mercer. You always stuttered? You have problems expressing yourself?

MERCER:

No. Sir.

COLONEL:

Good. Now, where did you get this idea? Did anybody
say anything to give you the impression that the
prisoner was to be mal-treated in any way?

MERCER:

I don't think so, sir.

COLONEL:

Your section commander, Sergeant Carrier? He say
anything?

MERCER:

I don't think so. No, sir.

COLONEL:

Lieutenant Broman? He say anything to that effect?
You telling me this comes from higher up, Trooper?

MERCER:

I couldn't say sir.

COLONEL:

Mercer, are you stupid or are you just pretending? You
said it was understood that prisoners were to be taught
a lesson.

MERCER:

I...nnmbelieve so sir.

COLONEL:

You believe so. How exactly was this understood?

MERCER:

Sir. I assumed, sir, that seeing as how—as how—
mmmng—h-h—the p-prisoner was being...ques-
tioned...by the others that it was all right.

COLONEL:

A 16 year old kid Mercer. He was beaten black and
blue. He was bound and beaten with a riot baton. Nine
teeth broken. Two ribs cracked. Index and middle
fingers of his left hand broken. Left foot crushed.
Human excrement dumped on his head. Cigarette
burns to forearms and pectorals and you assumed this
was all right? It was understood that this was all right?
Where the hell would you get that idea? You learn that
in basic? You learn that in cub scouts? Your father
teach you that?

Silence.

Answer the qu-qu-question Mercer.

MERCER:

No sir.

COLONEL:

You maybe aren't seeing things too clearly. I don't give
a shit who your daddy is, he's 11,000 kilometres away
anyhow. You are up to your goddamn eyeballs in some
heavy heavy shit and the only motherfucker can get
you out is me so you better start playing ball. Stop
trying to shit me. I'm your friend, you moron. I can
help you out of this mess, but don't you dare lie to me.

So, let's start again. What happened in that tent?

MERCER:

It was an accident sir. The gun—

COLONEL:

Accident? What? He was burned by accident? He broke
his foot by accident. Shit fell on his head by accident?
Don't jerk me around you pissy little insect. You fuck
me around anymore and I'll do everything in my

power to make sure that you don't get a court-martial. You'll get a civilian court and all kinds of press coverage and they will eat you alive. They will put you away for fucking ever. Do you understand what you're up on? Torture. 14 years. Manslaughter, if they don't nail you for murder. Kiss your life away.

Or maybe you're planning to save us all the trouble. You gonna do the same as Fortier when I turn my back? You planning on hanging yourself tonight?

I'll be honest. I look at you and Raymond and Fortier and I want to puke. You understand? You're a mess and you haven't even seen any action. You embarrass me. You insult the uniform, the forces, all the men who ever served. You're no better than a handful of fucking delinquent punks. Your whole platoon is unbalanced. You're a fucking disgrace Mercer. Combat? I wouldn't even assign you to peacekeeping duties. Shit, I wouldn't want you as a school crossing guard.

MERCER:
I wasn't there the whole time. I wasn't. They found him. They got him. Not me. I walked in on it.

COLONEL:
OK. What happened?

MERCER:
I heard all this noise, shouting, laughing, screaming like an animal. And I went in the tent. And I went in. And there was Sad—he was tied up his face all busted, bleeding and there's blood all over his eyes and he didn't see me. Didn't recognize me at first. I walked in and there he was. I couldn't nmbelieve it and I was just scared. I couldn't figure out what the fuck was going on. I just seen him. That afternoon and—and and and unng he was fine, everything was fine, he was like

always, he was like always and now there—bleeding and screaming.

I didn't want them to know. So I tried to make a joke out of it. Raymond he said my name, he said M-m—Mercer and then he heard it, he heard my name and—saw me then. He looked and saw me and he tried to call me, name, but his lips were too swollen or his broken teeth and he couldn't. I saw it, I saw, him trying, and he's there crying and nothing I could do. Raymond said, "watch this" and he hit him, hit mmmmng with the riot baton and Sa—Sa...he screamed, "Ca—Ca-Canada Canada Canada" and I, that's when I made the joke, I said, "Looks like a good trophy you got there." And Raymond said I should try it, so so so I did. I did. I hit him. I hit him, so, because. I hit him. I didn't know why was he there, nothing. I couldn't believe .

Then. I don't remember. It went on forever. It took forever. He was bleeding so much. No one came in, n-n-no officers. They said he was sneaking around the camp. He was trying to steal something. Nnmm—but that's not true. I mean it's not true. He came, I know why. He was curious, he was always curious. About the camp. He said he was gonna. Come. To see me. He—he—he told me before. I thought—kidding you know. I mean. I told him. He couldn't. He couldn't just come. I don't think he understood really why. He was just a kid.

COLONEL:
You knew him.

MERCER:
Yes. He—he saw me. He heard my name. He try to call...

COLONEL:

> He tried to call you but he couldn't. He was too badly beaten. Right. And you were scared. You didn't know what was going on. You were shocked to see him there.
>
> *A silence.*

Mercer?

> It was a terrible shock to see him there. You were frightened.
>
> *A silence.*

I know, it's a crazy fucking situation. World's gone fucking nuts Mercer. Things aren't what they used to be.

Canada's going to ratshit in a handbasket. Whole country's going to ratshit Mercer There's no political will.

Look at this situation, look at this.

Canada, we send our men, our equipment. What do we send? Three ships. Thirty years old. Ancient. Useless. What's the point? Supposed to have been modernized years ago. But no, Ottawa wants to save money. Send the men in to do a job but don't give 'em the equipment to do it with. It's nuts. It's criminal.

Oka. Christ what a nightmare. What a bloody nightmare. Just between you and me, right, 'cause I get the feeling you understand what I'm saying. You call in the army 'cause it's armed insurrection right? But do you let them do anything? No. You tie their hands. And the men stand there and take the shit and get garbage thrown at them and Indians point guns at them and they can't do anything but take it. Now, I ask you what is that? What is that Mercer? It's shit.

Let me tell you Mercer, sometimes, sometimes I think about chucking this whole thing. Still, I'm short time now. Might as well ride it out. Pension.

Oka. Oka Oka Oka. And the press? Jesus. A field day. The liberal press. The *Globe and Mail.* Feminist newspaper.

You read the papers Mercer?

I had a stroke a few years ago. This side of my body doesn't work as well as it did. I'm supposed to take it easy. Don't know how to. Never have, don't intend to start now. My doctor's worried I'll have another. My wife's worried I'll have a coronary. I figure when your number's up, your number's up. Till then you do what you gotta do.

Silence.

Shall we press on Mercer?

MERCER:
I told you. I told Lieutenant. I told everything. There's nnnnothing more. Why? I don't know why.

COLONEL:
I don't care about why Mercer. Why is for psychiatrists. The fact is it happened. I need to know details, how, when, who shot him.... Details.

How did you know him? How did you meet him?

MERCER:
I just did. I just met him. Sir.

COLONEL:
Where?

MERCER:
Out there.

COLONEL:
Where's that?

MERCER:
About a mmm…a mile from the base, sir. It's a place I
go to be alone.

COLONEL:
What happened?

MERCER:
Not much. We…uuh, talked. I'm thirsty. Sir?

COLONEL:
You talked. What about?

MERCER:
Don't remember sir. The heat. Canada.

COLONEL:
This Arab, he was just hanging—?

MERCER:
Uuumg…. Sadiq.

COLONEL:
Sadiq. That's his name?

MERCER:
Sadiq.

COLONEL:
What did you think of this Sadiq, Mercer? You liked
him? You like him? He give you anything?

MERCER:
No sir. I, uh, he was selling...he he he had...these...things to sell. I bought one.

COLONEL:
What?

MERCER:
No. N-n-nothing. Just...pictures.

COLONEL:
He was selling pictures. What kind of pictures?

MERCER:
Photographs.

COLONEL:
Photographs. You interested in photography Mercer?

MERCER:
Sometimes.

COLONEL:
These photographs? (pulls out SADIQ's envelope)

MERCER:
I don't know why I bought it.

COLONEL:
That's fine. I understand. You don't have to explain that to me. It's Jennifer isn't it? Your girlfriend?

MERCER:
Yes sir.

COLONEL:
Been a while since you've seen her.

MERCER:
Yes sir.

COLONEL:
Perfectly natural. Have some water. Help yourself.

So this guy is just peddling black market goods then.
He sell you anything else?

MERCER:
No. No sir.

COLONEL:
OK, so you meet this guy. He sells you some pictures.
You talk. Visiting. Cultural exchange like. I'm glad you
told me and nobody else needs to know about that.
You're doing real good. Just a few more questions.

MERCER:
What does it matter? Big deal? Who cares? He's n-n-
nobody. He's only a fucking Arab. That's what we're
here for. To kill a bunch of Arabs. He doesn't count.
He's here illegal anyway. Who needs to know?

COLONEL:
Mercer. We all have to agree. We need to be sure about
what happened that night. You understand? A lot of
people back home have questions about this. They
need some answers. Good answers. This isn't just about
your ass Mercer. Lot of asses on the line now.

Why did he come to the camp Mercer? What did he
want?

MERCER:
I told you. He was curious. That's all.

COLONEL:
Did he resist at all?

MERCER:
I wasn't there when they found him. I don't know what happened.

COLONEL:
He was shot in the back. Who shot him? It's important Mercer.

MERCER:
I don't know. I can't tell you anything. It's all mixed up. Nothing happened. I don't know anything. It can happen like that. It gets in. It gets in, in in and you're gone.

COLONEL:
What gets in Mercer?

Silence.

Son, I want you to know something. This is not a personal thing. It's just the way things are done. You understand. Professional. I don't say I approve. I say it's unfortunate.

It's stupid. It's all timing. Look, this guy died at the wrong time is all. In a day or two when the war breaks out, cause it will, trust me, if this guy got killed who the fuck'd know? Who'd care? Come on. It's fucking hypocrisy.

But there's a few more things. A few things that have got to be cleared up. Cause Raymond says you shot him. I don't believe him myself. But that's what he says. It looks like, you know, he was running away and that's why he's shot in the back. But by the time you got there this Sadiq he was in no condition to run was he?

89

That's what I thought. Why would Raymond lie to me?
You think he did it?

Silence.

I'll have to talk to Raymond some more. Tomorrow I
guess.

You can't keep it in forever Mercer.

What do you believe in? I was brought up Catholic
myself. I don't believe at all really but still I have this
suspicion, a doubt you know, that maybe there's something to all this about heaven and hell. Wouldn't that
be a fucking nightmare. If it was true? Eternity, eh.
Shit.

The funeral was in a church right? Must have been
strange.

What did you do while you were there? Hang out with
your father? Get some skiing in? Actually, I read the
psychiatrist's report. You went to that Eddie Murphy
movie the night after the funeral. What was the movie?
Another 48 Hours? I hear it's funny. Haven't seen it
myself.

You sure as shit aren't making my job any easier
Mercer.

What do you worry about Mercer?

He pulls out another envelope.

I got some other photographs here. Tell me about
these. That's Fortier there. That's Raymond. This must
be Sadiq. Who took these? Sixteen photographs here.
Who took them?

Silence.

All right Mercer, you don't want to talk? That's OK.
You can just nod your head. How's that? You don't
have to say a word.

You took them?

> *MERCER nods yes.*

COLONEL:
> Was it your idea? Raymond's idea?

> *MERCER nods yes.*

COLONEL:
> You sure about that?

> *MERCER nods.*

COLONEL:
> These supposed to be a joke? Like a safari or some-
> thing?

> *MERCER shrugs.*

COLONEL:
> Didn't you think? Didn't anybody think? The last thing
> we need is photographic evidence of this. You took
> this? This one here with the baton between his teeth
> and Fortier pulling him by the hair. You took this one?

> *MERCER nods.*

Was this before or after he was shot in the legs?

What about this one? Close-up of Sadiq's face with a
9mm. Browning shoved in his mouth. You take that?
You remember taking that?

> *MERCER nods yes.*

COLONEL:

You sure? Whose hand is this in the photo Mercer?

MERCER shrugs.

COLONEL:

Look close. Recognize that hand? Course you do. It's yours Mercer. Same ring. That's your hand holding your Browning in the Arab kid's mouth.

What are these pictures called? What is the common term in the regiment for this type of picture? It's called a hero picture isn't it? I've heard them described by everyone I've talked to as a hero picture. Picture's worth a thousand words, eh Mercer?

What do you feel when you look at that Mercer? You get off on it? You feel anything? Nothing at all? Like at your mother's funeral? Would you say there's something wrong with somebody who can't feel anything for his dead mother?

MERCER refuses to look at photo.

You getting confused Mercer, that's it. You need to see a shrink probably. You need psychiatric care? You're going mental like your mother, is that it?

Pause.

Where'd the camera come from?

Was it there in the tent?

MERCER shrugs.

Whose camera was it?

Silence.

Whose camera was it? Where'd you get the camera?

What the fuck do you think you're doing Mercer? You think you're smarter than me? What the fuck is your problem? Look at me, boy. You think you can get away with something here? You think somebody's going to remember you did them a favour by not talking?

Produces camera.

The camera you took the photos with belongs to Martin Broman. Do you know who that is? Who is that? Would that be Lieutenant Broman? Right. Lieutenant Broman. Your Platoon Commander.

COLONEL takes photo of MERCER. Flash.

OK. We'll put this shit away. Let's forget all this shit for now, OK? We forget the photos, you don't have to look at them anymore. I know it was Broman's camera. No big deal. I'll manage that.

It's Broman's fault. I know that. It's his responsibility. And I am going to make damned sure that this whole thing gets nailed to his sorry fat pimply queer ass.

OK, look, we trade OK? I told you. You tell me. Exchange. Fair trade. Fair enough.

An extremely long silence.

Did you shoot him Mercer? I know you hit him with the baton. Tell me Mercer, did you shoot him?

You can tell me. I understand these things. I volunteered in Vietnam, Mercer. U.S. Marines. So I have seen a thing or two myself. Close-up. I understand what can happen. Trust me. Help me out Mercer.

I know you can help me. You want to help me. Because you knew him. You were practically friends. We need to know what happened Mercer, so we can do something for his family. Right?

He must have had some family. He was somebody's kid. Sixteen, that's just a boy. You have to tell me, Mercer. So I can do something. So I can help them. So I can help you.

Mercer, I'm going to tell you something. A story.

We had these things, M-26 fragmentation grenades. V.C. used to rig them up, delay, drop one into the gas tank of a jeep and they'd blow the whole thing up good and proper. It was like ten grenades put together when you did that. I had two friends went that way. Bert and JP, they climbed into the jeep, swung it around, Bert was leaning on the horn and I was coming up the street towards them. I was unwrapping a pack of cigarettes and reaching for my lighter and I remember so clearly because when the jeep blew I was confused, I thought that my lighter had done it, somehow. But it was a flash. I watched it blow. Saw them fly apart.

All afternoon, there'd been this kid hanging out. He was ten, maybe older, little. Ten or twelve. He stuck with us all afternoon. He was laughing, making jokes, getting beer, asking questions. All afternoon. It must have been him, slipped it in the tank. You have to wonder what the hell it takes to make a ten year old blow up a jeep. That was the day of my nineteenth birthday. Every night that week I dream about boys coming up to me selling cigarettes and when I look it's a grenade.

It's a week after. We're coming upriver through these hamlets that've been neutralized. It's quiet as shit. We're tired as hell. We all just want to sit, rest, eat. We're poking around, slow, make sure the place is secure. I'm way out on the edge of the village, pretty far from everybody else. Standing in front of a hut, it's burned, still standing. All alone. I'm just staring at it, thinking about a shed we had out back at home that looks nothing like this one. There's a noise. Like coughing. So in I go. Very slow. Very quiet. There's somebody in the corner. A boy, he's maybe ten years old. I'm so tired I think I'm dreaming, hallucinating. He gets up. He starts to get up. I put a couple of shots in his legs. He falls. Screaming gook. I just stood there looking at him Mercer. Telling myself it's not the same kid. Then I put another one in his gut. And one more in his chest. Took him a long time to die.

Turned out he was blind. From the chemicals. Or whatever.

There was no reason to shoot him. I had no reason. He was unarmed, blind, a boy.

Just like the movies, eh Mercer? Kid goes to war, sees terrible things, ends up doing terrible things. Boo hoo. But all's fair in love and war and ain't it a crying shame?

Bullshit. Bull fucking shit.

It's not that simple.

We are a part of something Mercer. Something that asks us to do certain things, expects us to do certain things. You hear what I'm saying? We follow orders right? You've got your orders. I've got mine. But we agree to follow those orders. We make decisions, Mercer. We are a part of it. Look at us here in this tent. What the fuck are we doing? What's going on here? It's all a flaming pile of shit Mercer. And we're a part of it.

Mercer, listen. I made a decision when I killed that boy. I made a decision after. I became a professional soldier. I thought I'd put it behind me. I take the bus to work sometimes Mercer. But I still dream about kids with bombs for hearts.

I know.

MERCER:
I don't think you do sir.

COLONEL:
Then I'm asking you please to tell me.

MERCER:
You can't touch me now. Or him. Sadiq. It doesn't matter. It's over.

It gets in. It got in.

I kissed him. I sucked his cock. We—he. We fucked. He melted me like an explosion like a Big Blue 82. He evaporated who I was, disintegrated me. He put his hands on my stomach and that hole in my gut...he filled it up with his brown hands.

I broke his teeth. I cracked his ribs. I kissed his lips.

Put that in your report sir. There's nothing else. That's all. It's over.

Jets fly by again. Landing perhaps. The COLONEL slowly packs his brief case, speaks briefly to MERCER, though, again we cannot hear what he is saying. He exits, leaving MERCER alone in the tent. The generator putt-putts then, silence.

Scene Two

*MERCER in Vancouver. A phone rings and rings
and rings. MERCER regards it then finally
answers.*

MERCER:
Hello?

Jen. Hi.

I'm OK. You know. Bit surprised. I mean, I was thinking of calling you but I wasn't sure you'd want to. Talk
to me.

Pretty fucking weird. I don't know. I thought there'd
be a lot bigger deal in the papers and that but there
was hardly anything.

It was.... The desert was wild.

Not much. Lying low. Watching TV. Been going for
drives around. Down to the water and that. It's nice up
here. Quiet. Like always. I've got the house to myself.

How are you? How's school?

Good.

I don't know really. Just try and chill. Get my shit
together. I want to go back to Germany.

I'm just trying to take it one day at a time. Getting my
shit together.

Yeah well, something happened. It's over. I have to deal
with it and if other people want to be freaked out
about it that's their problem. Life goes on.

I'm not saying you. No.

A long pause.

Thanks. Thanks.

SADIQ appears.

Next week. I'm not into it right now. Coffee. Starbucks.
Next week. You're on.

OK. I'll call you. Monday or something.

I will. Promise.

You too. Bye

*MERCER hangs up phone. He does not
acknowledge SADIQ in any way.*

SADIQ:

Mercer. You cannot touch me now. I am too far. You
have left only pictures. Photographs. Can you see me?

I have surprise for you. Guess where I go? Not America,
Mercer. I am in Sudbury. Ontario. Canada. Cold. When
I come to my room it is full of clothes and parka. I am
wearing my new sweater. Stanfield's. Very nice, very
warm.

In Palestine, you know, boys like me, smaller too, throw
rocks. Intifada. Israeli soldiers come and break hands
of boys. Some boys die. Not just boys, everyone fight.
You think it is crazy but no. They have reasons for to
fight in Palestine, the mothers and fathers and
children and the children to come. They are fight for a
home, for to survive.

You come to Qatar to Kuwait Mercer. Why? Why you
fight here? Not only you, whole world. Come. Why?
You do not know, you go only where they tell you.

Who tell you to hit me Mercer? Why you burn me? Do
you know what reason? He break my foot, the big one,
blonde hair straight. You say nothing. Do nothing. I ask
why for what reason?

You are no reason. You are an animal, you Canadian peacekeeper, you are shit, a beast. If I could reach that gun, I would like to kill you and all your friends. He deserve to die, that one hang himself. You too.

You tell me of Canada and your father and you lonely and the hole in you. You hurt. You cry. Do you cry for me Mercer? Who cry for me? My family, sisters and mother and father too. But they do not matter to you. Death mean little to us you say. But no. We laugh like you. We bleed like you. We die like you. We deserve to life like you.

Now.

Now. Everything is different. The bruises and burns. They are gone. I am new again. Forgetting. Time. Not forgive. No. But I do not wish harm to you. I have only one picture of you Mercer. I see you as little boy.

When I go to base that night I tell them I am looking for a child. It is our secret.

Today, I am very hungry. I have my first donut, I sneak in the back of Tim Horton's. Long john. I think if I am not the way I am, dead, it would make me very sick, Military Man.

I miss the sun, the heat. Here everything is clear.

End.

99

What follows is the original second act which was eventually cut from the play when it was produced at the New Play Centre in Vancouver in April of 1995. It is enclosed here as an alternate second act.

Act Two

Scene One

NORMAN:

Hello, my name is Norman. Welcome to the Border Project.

Welcome, one and all. Welcome male and female. Welcome homos, lesbos, bi- and heterosexual. Welcome those who are celibate—by choice or circumstance.

Welcome atheist, agnostic and new ageist. Welcome Protestant, Catholic and Jew. Welcome Muslim. Welcome Hindu, welcome Buddhist and welcome Shinto.

Welcome conservative, liberal, and person left of centre. Welcome Natural Law Party voter. Welcome if you sell the Socialist Worker at First and Commercial on Saturdays. Welcome even to those who voted Reform.

Welcome tree-hugger and tree cutter, recycler and cyclist. Welcome eco-feminist worshipper of the god-dess. Welcome godless corporate despoiler of nature's bounty. Welcome real woman and drum beating new-man. Welcome to those who know what you were in past lives

Vegetarian and vegan, omnivore and carnivore: welcome. Riot grrrl and neo-hippie, body-piercer and/or scarifier; tattoo artist and tattoo bearer: welcome.

Bienvenue cat, dog, ferret, or bird lover. Welcome nail biter and nose picker. Welcome to you who enjoy farting in the bath tub.

Welcome smoker. Welcome non.

Welcome the kind of guy who peels the label off beer bottles leaves a little pile of shreds on the table.

Landlord, tenant, hacker, phreak and nerd, cyber punk and beach bum, breast-feeding mother and full time father: welcome welcome welcome.

Welcome northerner, southerner, easterner and westerner. Welcome white, welcome black, welcome red, yellow and brown. Welcome Angle and Saxon, Celt and Gaul, Latin and African, Arab, Jew, Persian, Asian, First Nation, Indo-European, Mediterranean and Kiwi. Welcome.

To the Border Project.

And this evening, The Border Project is very pleased to welcome as our guest, actor and playwright, the author of *A Line in the Sand*, Mr. Marcus Youssef.

MARCUS:
January 16, 1991. The day I'd been waiting for: the expiration of the US's ultimatum to Saddam to get the hell out of Kuwait, or else. I'm glued to my radio and they interrupt *As it Happens* and tell me—well, not just me, a lot of other people, but it feels like just me because I'm alone in my apartment—they tell me or else has started. Their voices are excited, energized. This is news: important, up to the minute, in your face

—even though it's half way across the world—kind of news.

Half. That's what I am. Half Arab. Half Egyptian. In this war, Egypt's on our side. Hell, I'm North American. My Dad, the real Arab, hates the place. I don't speak a word of Arabic. I haven't lived with my father since I was 15; didn't even know the name of his place of birth until about eight months ago; had always assumed he was from Cairo. I mean, where else is there in Egypt?

But by blood, by heritage, by faith, I feel like an Iraqi. Like an Arab.

Early reports from the Pentagon, my radio friend tells me, are of overwhelming success. Targets have been hit, no coalition planes lost, minimal collateral damage.

We are killing people who look like me.

When they tell me that Baghdad looks beautiful—lit up like Christmas or the Fourth of July—I chew at my thumbnail until it bleeds then grab at the phone to contact him, my father, the Arab, so I can remember, remind myself that I am not alone.

But when my dad's girlfriend answers the phone, she is hysterical. Tells me my father has collapsed. She's waiting for the ambulance. Thinks he's having a heart attack. He saw the report of an Iraqi chemical weapons attack on CNN and that was it. He passed out. Stopped breathing.

My father was born in the biblical city of Quesna, where Christ transformed water into wine. And now, imagining he will die—at this instant—I am irrevocably transformed into an Arab.

NORMAN:
Marcus Patrick Youssef: Arab.

NORMAN motions to lighting booth.

*Audio/Video: Opening sequence from the Disney
motion picture,* Aladdin. *"Arabian Nights."*

NORMAN:
Did you see Aladdin, Marcus?

MARCUS:
Yes, yes I did.

NORMAN:
Wasn't Robin Williams great?

MARCUS:
He was OK.

NORMAN:
You know he improvised all that stuff, eh? The
animators, they just followed whatever he made up.

MARCUS:
Actually, Norman, I have to say that as an Arab I found
the movie quite problematic. I mean, it was released
barely a year after the Gulf War had ended. And they
changed the lyrics of that opening song for the video
release. It used to be, "Oh, I come from a land, from a
faraway place, where the caravan camel's roam. Where
they cut off your ear if they don't like your face, it's
barbaric but, hey, it's home."

NORMAN:
Marcus Patrick Youssef: Serious about cartoons.

So, Marcus, this Gulf War thing, it really gets you, doesn't it? Why? What's the big deal?

MARCUS:

It was a scam. A pack of lies. A criminal act of monumental proportions. We were led to believe that the total destruction of Iraq's national infrastructure, not to mention the deaths of thousands and thousands of people was the necessary consequence of a noble defence of freedom. I believe four facts will underline the fundamental hypocrisy at the heart of this war.

NORMAN:

Facts. Such as?

MARCUS:

1) Saddam Hussein was a Western ally for many years, even though we knew he had a terrible human rights record. Throughout the 1980's Western governments provided him with money and arms to fight Iran, despite the fact that he was using chemical weapons against the Kurds.

2) Before and during the war there were at least 6 different peace proposals put forward by different parties, including one Iraqi offer of unconditional withdrawal, all of which were rejected by the US. Yet we were constantly told that all diplomatic options had been exhausted.

3) Some 150,000 Iraqis were killed and 300,000 wounded. American casualties were 146, 60 of whom were killed by friendly fire. This was no war, it was a slaughter.

4) The Gulf War was the testing and demonstration ground for a whole new generation of conventional

weaponry designed to reproduce the effects of nuclear weapons without using nuclear components.

NORMAN:
For example?

MARCUS:
For example, Fuel Air Explosives—the development of which was researched at McGill University—Fuel Air Explosives like the Big Blue 82. Which is a massive 15,000 pound exploding fireball which moves at a rate of 1,825 meters per second. If one were dropped, right now, on Performance Works, Granville Island—*(slaps hands together)* poof.

NORMAN:
Marcus Patrick Youssef: Knowledgeable Guy

Scene Two

NORMAN:
And this Gulf War stuff means so much to you that
you've actually gone and written a play about it.

MARCUS:
Actually, it's not about the Gulf War, it's set in the Gulf
War. I felt that the Gulf War was a really concrete
example of how cultural stereotypes and propaganda
can convince us to accept the wholesale slaughter of
other human beings.

NORMAN:
Hunh. Now, Marcus, it's called a *Line in the Sand*, right?

MARCUS:
That's right.

NORMAN:
'Cause you know the first time I heard it, I thought it
was a *Lion in the Sand*.

MARCUS:
Oh, yeah.

NORMAN:
Thought it was by Judith Thompson.

MARCUS:
Right.

NORMAN:
Now, is this play as important as it seems?

MARCUS:
Well, I don't think I'm really in a position to judge.

NORMAN:
So tell us about the play.

MARCUS:
Well, it's the story of a Canadian soldier stationed in the Persian Gulf just before the outbreak of hostilities and the relationship he develops with a 16 year old Palestinian.

NORMAN:
How do you think it went?

MARCUS:
I thought it was pretty good. Energy was up there. Cam was great, and Vince really comes through for us in the third act. My original inspiration for the story was *L'etranger* by Albert Camus, a novel about a Frenchman who kills an Arab—an Arab who has no name, no history and no voice. The story's other source is the torture and murder of a 16 year old Somali boy named Shidane Arone. You may remember he was killed by Canadian soldiers on a UN humanitarian mission in Somalia in March of 1993.

NORMAN:
Which you've transposed to the Gulf War.

MARCUS:
Right.

NORMAN:
Because you're an Arab.

MARCUS:
I don't know. I guess you could say that.

NORMAN:
Well, aren't you? What about your mother?

MARCUS:
What about her?

NORMAN:
Is she 'Arabian'?

MARCUS:
Well, no. My parents met in Berkeley, California. My father was on an exchange program from the University of Cairo. My mum was an undergrad from Bakersfield.

NORMAN:
Bakersfield?

MARCUS:
Yeah.

NORMAN:
Right on the edge of the Mojave desert there.

MARCUS:
That's right.

NORMAN:
Isn't that where they shot *Every Which Way But Loose?* You know, that Clint Eastwood movie. The one with the monkey?

MARCUS:
I don't know.

NORMAN:

I have relatives in Topanga. So what's with all the
pornography in the play, Marcus? What's that about?

MARCUS:

Well, the idea for that came from a *New York Times*
article, actually, from during the Gulf War that said
American pilots were being shown pornographic
movies before flying bombing sorties over Iraq.

NORMAN:

Do you know that Canadian soldiers had it as well?

MARCUS

No, but if the antics of the airborne are anything to go
by, it's not hard to imagine that they would.

NORMAN:

Do you ever look at pornography?

MARCUS:

That's a very personal question, Norman.

NORMAN:

I thought that's what we're talking about here. You.

MARCUS:

I'm afraid I have to plead the fifth on that one,
Norman.

NORMAN:

I see.

So it must have been hard, eh, Marcus? Growing up an
Arab in North America.

MARCUS:

Well, yes, Norman. Since you mention it, sometimes it was.

NORMAN:

Please, tell us about it.

Scene Three

MARCUS:

My name is Marcus Patrick Youssef and I speak hieroglyphics.

Summer camp. Every year. I used to claim that I was the great, great, great, great and thirty seven more greats grandson of Tutankhamen. All the little white kids would ask, "Like, really?" and I'd go, "Well, no, I mean, we were probably the guys who built the pyramids."

When I was marching in a demonstration against the Gulf War in Montreal, right in the middle of the street this young woman taps me on the shoulder and says, "We're not for Saddam either, you know."

Picture of MARCUS' face

Picture of MARCUS' back.

Look at my skin.

Ladies and Gentlemen, this is an Arab's skin. It needs heat, sunlight, aridity. Look what happens to Semitic skin when it's transported to the cool moistness of the northwest temperate rain forest.

And you know what causes acne, don't you? I've looked it up. Excess production of oil. And who produces oil? Arabs.

And this, look at this. (*creates pile of dandruff*). I have to use Denorex shampoo to keep my scalp together. It's ten percent tar. Ten percent. Tar. And you know where tar comes from: Oil. And you know who produces oil? Right.

My nose. Look at my nose.

Picture of MARCUS' nose.

Here, we have what is commonly referred to as a
"Roman Nose." But as should already be fairly obvious,
I am not Roman. And this particular olfactory organ
belongs to me. Therefore, by the transitive property,
this is not a Roman nose.

When I was a kid—don't look at me like that, Norman
one more personal story isn't going to kill anyone—
when I was a kid, Norman, in high school, I used to
complain—a lot like now, I guess—about how ugly I
thought my nose was, and my friends always used to tell
me, "But you've got a Roman Nose." It suits your face,
they told me. It suits your face. That suits my face?
What does this say about my face?!

Because we all know that so-called Roman Noses are
ugly. They look ridiculous. They protrude from the
face, disembodied, out of proportion, and, worst of all,
their great aesthetic tragedy, they curve. There is
nothing uglier than a curved nose. Except, of course, a
big, curved nose.

Picture of a "button" nose.

This nose. Is what is commonly referred to as a
"button" nose. We like this nose. I like this nose. It's
Karen Turner's nose. It's cute. Safe. Endearing. It's a
nose I'd like to ask out on a date but be afraid of going
too quickly and frightening away or putting into a
compromised position. This nose demands a long, slow
courtship. A month of flowers, tissues and sniffs about
allergies and Sudafed. Then, maybe dissolve some
cocaine into its nasal spray and you might get what
you're really after. Don't you just want to corrupt it—
knowing, of course, that secretly, deep in it's nasal cavi-
ty, it must really want you to.

Before this ugly metaphor goes any further I'd like to ask Norman to read something that may help contextualize this whole little episode. This quote is taken from a book called *The Arab Mind Considered: A Need for Understanding.*[19]

Go ahead, Norman.

NORMAN:
"Because of the frustrations and repressions which follow from the rigidly held sexual mores and prohibitions of his own society, the Arab is dangerous to women of other nationalities. Many Western girls working for big companies with branches in Arab countries have been indecently assaulted or raped. It is impossible for a woman to walk down a public street at night without serious risk. Arab men in groups are constantly on patrol in their own cars, watching for such prey, in cities such as Beirut and Tripoli."

MARCUS:
Unquote.

We can assume then that the American's 1982 bombardment of Beirut, the Gulf War, and those Tomahawk missiles Bill Clinton dropped on Baghdad are all part of a top secret, US military campaign to ensure the safety of expatriate American females. Satellites now track Arabic men as they drive down Arabic city streets, and at the first suggestive glance at a woman with a US passport, two or three F-111's scramble to teach us woman-hating Arabs a lesson. After all, we all know how safe and secure North American women are late at night on their own city streets.

NORMAN:
Marcus Patrick Youssef: Hard Done By.

NORMAN motions to the lighting booth.

Video Sequence: Excerpt from Aladdin, *"One Jump Reprise."*

Scene Four

MARCUS:
  Ha, ha. That's very funny.

NORMAN:
  You take this all pretty seriously don't you?

MARCUS:
  Yes, I do.

NORMAN:
  You're kind of touchy about this Arab stuff—

MARCUS:
  I wouldn't say touchy, exactly, I would say justifiably—

NORMAN:
  Where were you born, exactly?

MARCUS:
  Um, Queen Elizabeth Hospital. Montreal.

NORMAN:
  Montreal, Canada?

MARCUS:
  Yes, it's still part of Canada, last time I looked.

NORMAN:
  And how many times did you say you've been to the
  Middle East?

MARCUS:
  Uh, never.

NORMAN:
Right. And you don't speak Arabic?

MARCUS:
That's correct.

NORMAN:
Now your father, born in Egypt, he used to work for
the Royal Bank, right?

MARCUS:
Yes. Why?

NORMAN:
What was his position there?

MARCUS:
Uh, senior executive vice-president.

NORMAN:
Whoo—guess he got his own desk, huh?

MARCUS:
Ha, ha.

NORMAN:
What was he making, like 80, 90 grand?

MARCUS:
Something like that.

NORMAN:
And what's he up to these days, Marcus?

MARCUS:
Uh, well, he's a part owner of a pension management
company.

NORMAN:
Part owner.

So, financially speaking, Canada hasn't exactly
oppressed your father, has it, Marcus? You haven't
exactly suffered here?

MARCUS:
No, for sure. Yes, Norman, I am in no way attempting
to say—

NORMAN:
Now, is it true that throughout your pre-teen and
teenage years you watched *MASH* religiously.

MARCUS:
Yes, I loved *MASH.*

NORMAN:
And *Different Strokes.*

MARCUS:
Uh, yeah.

NORMAN:
Starring Gary Coleman.

MARCUS:
Yes.

NORMAN:
And was the first record album you ever listened to
with some devotion your mother's copy of *Helen Reddy's
Greatest Hits?*

MARCUS:
Uh, yeah.

NORMAN:

On which your undisputed favourite song was "I am Woman Hear Me Roar."

MARCUS:

Yes.

NORMAN:

Did you not at one time own every book in the twenty four volume Walter Farley juvenile fiction series, *The Black Stallion?*

MARCUS:

Yes, I read a lot as a kid.

NORMAN:

And did you not spend most every minute in the two months leading up to Christmas, age 9-13 offering to trade your soul to the devil if your parents bought you an Atari home video console?

MARCUS:

Yeah. I was desperate for Space Invaders.

NORMAN:

On January 12, 1981, in the shower of your house on 510 Tatum Drive did you or did you not have your first extended pre-pubescent sexual fantasy.

MARCUS:

Yes, I did.

NORMAN:

About Lady Diana.

MARCUS:

Yeah.

NORMAN:

    Marcus, I hate to blow holes in your little theory here but you sound to me like a totally assimilated, enculturated young North American. A perfectly average, if somewhat over-privileged, maybe a bit fucked up, but entirely North American. Just where do you get off calling yourself Arab? Preaching to me about the Gulf War?

MARCUS:

    Well, it's a complicated question. First of all, Norman, I don't think I preached to you about the Gulf War. I think I gave you four facts about the Gulf War.

NORMAN:

    Marcus Patrick Youssef.

    Raised in upper middle class suburbs all over the world—

    Educated at private International schools in Europe and Queen's University—

    Given a standard of living 98% of his Canadian compatriots will never know—

    Calls himself an Arab.

    Marcus Patrick Youssef. Hypocrite.

MARCUS:

    Norman, I don't think it's just a—

NORMAN:

    You thought this was going to be a little forum for you to have an identity crisis didn't you? An opportunity to tell a few personal stories and explore your shattered self. I guess you thought we'd all just sit around quietly and let you go on and on about your sense of loss, your confusion, your uniqueness, your singular experience as an Arab-Canadian. And eventually, you'd accuse us all of racism and complain about mainstream culture and how it doesn't accommodate you, how it oppresses you and your kind. You want us to feel guilty about going to war against some brutal dictator who invaded a small, defenceless country. Of course, you wouldn't put it like that. You'd do it artfully, subtly. But it all comes down to the same thing in the end doesn't it?

Well forget it, Marky Marcuse.

Because I for one have had enough whining and moaning from you and people like you about your special little problems and your special little anxieties. Get a life. Go back to Egypt. Get with the program, pal. The Gulf War ended 4 years ago. There are bigger problems, now. You ever hear about the deficit ?

Interest rates?

The crime problem?

Scene Five

MARCUS:
>   Like I tried to say before, Norman. It's complicated.
>   It's not just about economics.

NORMAN:
>   What's it about then? CULTURE?!?

MARCUS:
>   Well, yes. Partially.

NORMAN:
>   This is your culture, Marcus. We are your culture. Like
>   it or not.

MARCUS:
>   Why are you so upset about this, Norman?

NORMAN:
>   I want you to face some facts. Reality check. Admit it.
>   There is nothing special about you. This play you
>   wrote. What does all that foot rubbing have to do with
>   being an Arab. You trying to tell me that your nose
>   makes you an Arab? Your skin? That's it? That's all you
>   have to go on? Plenty of people out there with big
>   noses, Marcus. Lots of folks with acne out there, you
>   don't see them getting all self-righteous about the Gulf
>   War and claiming kinship with Omar Khayam.

MARCUS:
>   Look, it's complicated. I'm not sure I can explain it.
>   It's just something I feel.

NORMAN:
>   You feel you're an Arab?

MARCUS:

Yes. Sometimes.

NORMAN:

And other times?

MARCUS:

I don't. When I happily pay eight dollars to see *True Lies*. When I read the word "terrorist" in the Globe and Mail and think of Yasser Arafat. When they tell me, minimal collateral damage and I imagine a giant video game. When they talk about surgical air strikes and I forget that Baghdad is not diseased, that bombs do not navigate cities like scalpels bodies. When I forget and I believe. Then, yes, I guess you're right, Norman. In spite of my skin and my nose and my name, then I'm just like you. North American. Or forget—

NORMAN:

Marcus, you worry. He worries about this Arab-Canadian thing. He wonders why he gets so worked up about wars in the Middle East and if he has any right to call himself an Arab at all. Don't you?

He worries.

I don't. I'm a lot like you, out there. I'm normal. I'm average. I'm a responsible tenant. I recycle. I don't worry about who I am. I shower regularly. I put money in the bank for emergencies, taxes and car insurance: I'm a lot like you. I'm uncircumcised and glad. I watch TV, not a lot, but some. I think about joining Amnesty International. When I'm lonely, I smoke or masturbate. When my father died, I felt relieved. I'm a lot like you. Normal.

But Marcus, he worries. He worries when he studies photographs of his father as a young man; when he reads novels by Naguib Mafhouz; when he daydreams of Alexandria and an audience with the Coptic Pope.

MARCUS:
You want to know why I am North American? Because when I look in the mirror I don't recognize my own face. It doesn't look like me.

NORMAN:
Marcus, you need to relax. Take it easy. Kick back. Don't take everything so seriously. This is Vancouver, dude.

I feel for you, Marcus. It's hard.

Hook-nosed Arabic on the outside, and 100% pure, cholesterol-free, smooth talking, quick thinking, over-achieving Californian on the inside.

Marcus, everything you need is right here: look deep into your soul. Remember the teller of tales from your youth, the maker of Mickey, the Donald of Duck. For to this dilemma we have an answer, a solution, Mr. Marcus Patrick Youssef, look up,

MARCUS:
Up?

NORMAN:
To the fantasy of *Fantasia*, the God of Sunday Evening at 6:00, the hour before 60 minutes. In the Wit of Walt, the Dynasty of Disney, we have found your saviour—

MARCUS:
You mean?

NORMAN:
Go on, Marcus. It won't hurt a bit. It's just a cartoon.

Marcus Patrick Youssef: ALADDIN!

Video: "Prince Ali" sequence excerpts from
Aladdin.

MARCUS:
(weeping and wailing and gnashing his teeth) I AM
ALADDIN!

He falls to his knees.

*Video: "Whole New World" Magic Carpet Ride
from* Aladdin *on first monitor with Gulf air war
excerpts over Baghdad on second monitor.*

Endnotes

1. This speech is taken from *Hansard* for January 16, 1991.

2. *High-Death Weapons* by Michael T. Klare, originally published by The Nation Magazine /The Nation Co. Inc., June 3, 1991. Reprinted in *It Was, It Was Not*, ed. Mordecai Briemberg, New Star Books, Vancouver, 1992, p. 46.

3. *High-Death Weapons*, Michael T. Klare, p.46.

4. Indonesia invaded East Timor on December 7, 1975, ten days after East Timor declared its independence from Portugal. At least 200,000 people, representing 1/3 of the population of East Timor, have died as a result of the Indonesian occupation. Indonesia is a core recipient of Canadian aid. See also: Noam Chomsky's *Year 501: The Conquest Continues*, Black Rose Books, Montreal, 1993.

5. Starring Arnold Schwarzenegger, a well-known Republican, and seen by millions representing a multitude of political persuasions.

6. Authors' estimates.

7. After much public pressure, these lyrics were changed.

8. This is standard rhetoric and of course, completely untrue. There were numerous attempts from different parties to negotiate a peaceful end to the conflict. All of these efforts were blocked by the US and, with few exceptions, dutifully ignored by mainstream media. See: *Journal of Palestine Studies*, Volume

XX, Number 3, Spring 1991. See also: *Desert Shield to Desert Storm* by Dilip Hiro, HarperCollins, 1992.

9.   A Harvard medical team that visited Iraq stressed a direct correlation between bombing damage to Iraqi infrastructure (power generating plants, for example) and the breakdown of public health (contaminated water supplies etc.). They estimated that at least 150,000 children under the age of five would die from infectious diseases in the 12 month period following the cessation of bombing. (*Globe and Mail*, May 22, 1991) According to the U.N., on-going sanctions against Iraq have resulted in approximately half a million deaths.

10. This story was brought to us by Hill and Knowlton, the PR firm hired by the Kuwaiti government after the Iraqi invasion. See among others, *Public Relations* by Johan Carlisle, *Covert Action*, Spring 1993, Number 44, p.19.

11. "Ottawa Sending CF-18 Fighter Jets," *Vancouver Sun*, Sept. 15, 1990.

12. "Forces' Hardware Geared for Defence," *Vancouver Sun*, Jan. 16, 1991.

13. From Stephen Dale's "Guns 'n Poses, The Myths of Canadian Peacekeeping," *This Magazine* Mar—Apr 1993, Vol. 26 No. 7, p.12.

14. The West has supported, in various ways, despots: Siad Barre of Somalia, Saddam Hussein of Iraq, King Fahd of Saudi Arabia, Amir al-Ahmad al-Sabah of Kuwait, among others.

15. See "Adding Humanitarian Intervention to the US Arsenal" by Alex de Waal and Rakiya Omaar in

Covert Action, Spring 1993 No. 44, p. 4; "Gravy Train: Feeding Pentagon by Feeding Somalia" by Stephen Shalom in *Z,* Feb. 1993 Vol. 6, No. 2, p.15; and "Somalia: The Cynical Manipulation of Hunger" by Mitchel Cohen in *Z,* Nov. 1993 Vol. 6, No. 11, p.33.

16. US Government estimates.

17. Stephen Dale, "Guns 'n Poses," p.16. Also graffiti on McGill campus.

18. *High-Death Weapons,* Michael T. Klare, p.47.

19. Laffin, John, *The Arab Mind Considered: A Need for Understanding,* New York, Talpinger Co., 1975.